THE MIRACLES OF FAITH.

A SKETCH OF THE LIFE OF

BEATÈ PAULUS.

BY
MARY WEITBRECHT.

WITH AN INTRODUCTION BY
REV. CHARLES S. ROBINSON, D.D.,
OF NEW YORK.

NEW YORK:
DODD & MEAD, NO. 762 BROADWAY.
1872.

CONTENTS.

INTRODUCTION.

The manuscript of this unpretending little volume fell into my hands in London. I brought it with me, and read it carefully on the sea.

The story brings before us one of those most attractive and beautiful characters we sometimes meet with in real life; a faithful Christian woman whose entire existence seemed to be lost in the will and wisdom of God. In a trust, fairly childlike, she rested unbrokenly. Some of the incidents here related have moved me much. I have not the pleasure of a personal acquaintance with the gifted lady who has written the narrative; but I am assured that in every particular it is positively true.

There never will be a deeper mystery in this world than that involved in the simplest and first exercise of prayer. How the eternal God can seem to leave anything whatsoever contingent on the requests of his creatures, passes philosophy. And that He goes so far in his offer as to say plainly, ASK AT WILL, is full of unutterable meaning. Now if one may gird up his faith, and rest assured that any petition he puts up is surely going to be answered, there seems little left to be desired for him.

This delightful little woman, dwelling chirk and cheerful on the borders of the Black Forest, believed God implicitly. She lived in the presence of the awful King of Heaven; yet never abashed, even while always reverent, she moved joyously forward among the sorrows and great perplexities of a more than usually burdened life. Her answers received, as she prayed, were wonderful.

Oh, there cannot be too much of this! God is our Father. Let us believe in him.

This sketch is delightfully written. I have very cordially consented to see it safely through the press. I sincerely hope, and believe, it will help many a true Christian to rest unquestioningly and unqualifiedly on the truth of this one verse :

"IF YE ABIDE IN ME, AND MY WORDS ABIDE IN YOU,

"YE SHALL ASK WHAT YE WILL, AND IT SHALL BE DONE INTO YOU !"

CHAS. S. ROBINSON,

Memorial Church, New York.

April 30, 1872.

THE MINISTER'S DAUGHTER.

"WHO THROUGH FAITH OBTAINED PROMISES."

Such was the Apostle's assertion, and his day did not close the long list of saints, faithful and true, who took God at His word, and gained glorious, though noiseless victories, by clinging to the Covenant of truth, which cannot be broken. Among the poor and hidden ones of earth, these grand witnesses to God's faithfulness have often dwelt apart. Now and then, one shines out in public life, to make the world wonder, and ask, as of old they did about the Master: "Whence hath this man these things?"

The following pages contain a narrative of facts, which to some may seem too strange, and to others, too insignificant, to be worthy of record. But to such as believe that God takes the truth, concealed from the wise of this world, and reveals it unto babes and simple folk, the story will bring a message of encouragement and good cheer.

Only a few years ago, there lived in a remote village in the South of Germany, a humble and devoted woman, the whole course of whose history bore a thrilling testimony to the might which still clings to a living faith. In order to trace the motive power of her life to its source, we must, after the fashion of German biographers, wander back among the chronicles of her family.

About one hundred years ago, any one chancing

to find himself upon the dusty high road, between the villages of Karnwestheim and Münchingen, in the early afternoon of a summer Sabbath, would have come upon a large concourse of country people, briskly trudging along through the hot sunshine. Youths and maidens, old men, and staid peasant matrons—in fact, a walking congregation—and in the midst of them, an earnest, holy messenger of Christ, who was their pastor. After attending morning worship, and the subsequent catechetical service in their own village, these hard-featured sons and daughters of toil would cheerfully set out in the wake of their valued minister, to go and listen to his sermon in the far off parish church of his father-in-law Flattich, a distance of several miles. The congregation at Münchingen had meanwhile assembled, and often sang through several of the heart-stirring German chorals, whilst awaiting their favorite preacher.

This pastor Halm is described to us as a man of great devotion and power, exerting a remarkable influence both in and out of the pulpit. It was not his clear and well developed method of thought, or the gift of eloquence which he possessed in marked degree, that made the common people throng after him, and listen so gladly and intently to the Word of life from his lips. A dignified appearance added to these talents, no doubt, and gave weight to his discourse; but that which made him mighty to sound forth the love and glory of our Lord, and of His Christ, was the grace of the Holy Spirit, "the author and giver of life."

"As he stood before us"—said a competent judge, in later years, to his grandson—"his face almost transfigured with its expression of high unearthly light, we no longer felt as if listening to a mere man. Our hearts heard the voice of one whom God had entrusted with a message, straight from His own presence." Great was the joy spread abroad in a place, when the news reached it that Pastor Halm was coming to preach. The tidings travelled like wildfire, and everyone crowded to listen and share the blessing. It was the hallowed influence of men such as this, that effectually counteracted the flood of ritualistic free thinking, which threatened to destroy the spiritual life of Germany during the last century.

Such is the account which reaches us, of the father of Beaté Paulus, a woman who proved not unworthy of her saintly parentage. The holy reverence in which she held his memory, may be gathered from an oft-repeated saying of her own children, when they noticed the eager delight with which on a free Sunday hour, she pored over the rich legacy of Halm's Sermons. "Mother," the little ones would naively exclaim, "the first seat in your heart is the dear Saviour's, but the very next is kept for your blessed father!" It is one of these children who, in graphic language, gives us the details of his mother's bright career, and as far as may be, we will adhere to the words in which he tells them.

It may be well to anticipate the surprise that some portions of the story may elicite in American readers, by reminding them of the almost patriarchal simplicity, and primitive manners of the country of which Madame Paulus was a native.* The position of woman there

* Winttemberg, a small Kingdom in South Germany.

differs widely from that which she occupies with us, while at the same time, it is quite usual to find high, intellectual culture co-existing with modes of life which to us seem almost uncivilised in their severe hardihood.

CHAPTER I.

The Pastor's Wife.

It would not be easy to find a married pair differing so widely from each other, as did our father and mother. The latter being a daughter and grand-daughter of men alike noted for piety and originality of mind, felt at home in a sphere of thought dealing with subjects of revealed truth, and higher life of communion with God, together with the practice of Christian charity. My father on the other hand, belonged to a family, some of whose members had attained to wordly distinction, one of them being a noted rationalist; hence his interest lay chiefly in intellectual and scientific research, and the enjoyment of social intercourse.

Notwithstanding this marked dissimilarity our parents were united in hearty affection, mutual admiration and respect characterising their relations. Although differing from the views held by his wife, our father regarded her convictions as sacred, and venerated in her a high spiritual life in which he was not a sharer. As a child, I remember his calling me to a window to witness two pious clergymen approaching our parsonage. "Look, little Philip," said he; "there are two servants of God." When in the course of subsequent conversation they asked him whether any "pietists" lived in the parish, "Certainly, and not a few," was his prompt reply. Surprised, they inquired the number. "Thirty," he said; and noticing their wondering looks, added playfully—"Well, you see, there is my wife, who counts for twenty-four in her own person, and six other women hold with her, heart and soul!"*

For ten years our parents had thus lived very happily together, and were now located at Astelsheim, a village near Calw in the Black Forest, where my father's genial temper united to our mother's unfailing kindness, had won the hearts of the simple peasants around them. The exceptionally fine vintage of the year 1811 had filled our country with rejoicings, and it was in the midst of this pleasant excitement that our mother sickened, and was soon prostrated by nervous fever. In the middle of one night, our father hurriedly sent for his brother, a physician in practice at Stuttgart, for our village doctor began to despair of coping with

* Pietists is a term of reproach in Germany, applied to any spiritual and earnest Christians.

the disease. Our uncle came in haste, bringing with him a female cousin, who found plenty of work in nursing and the care of six small children under the age of ten. No one besides was in the house, except our old grandmother, and the offers of help made by kind but inexperienced neighbors availed little. Uncle Carl startled our poor father terribly, by declaring that recovery would be possible only in one such case out of a hundred, and consternation spread through the village with the sad tidings of our impending loss, for her constant sympathy and kindness had endeared the sufferer to a surprising extent. Our grandmother alone remained calm and collected amid the general lamentation. For long ago she had passed through God's school of sorrow, in the early death of her husband and three highly-gifted children just reaching maturity. Under such circumstances she had learned to sacrifice her own will to a higher and Divine one.

The illness had now lasted for a week, and we were anxiously awaiting the crisis. Vainly the little children gathered round the sick bed, entreating their mother in imploring tones, not to go away and leave them. Increasing weakness showed us that death was rapidly approaching, and mournfully our grandmother commenced the sad though needful preparation for the end. By degrees, the room became crowded with villagers who, having heard the rumor of the Frau Pastorin's expected death, longed to have a farewell word from her lips. With his face hidden in his hands, our father stood by the side of his wife in dumb anguish, and behind crowded the children, sobbing and wringing their hands in terror and a helpless longing to hold back the parting spirit. It was a touching sight, and many tears were shed by those who looked upon it. Only one soul in all the company was calm, and did not weep ; that was the mother herself. For she believed that all her toil was over, and being ready to die, nothing remained for her but to say good-bye. So she fixed her fading eyes once more upon her husband, and drawing him to her with trembling hands, kissed him, as for the last time ; she then beckoned the children to her side and caressed them ; finally, making a sign to those around her, she gave her hand to each in turn, and then in a faint voice murmured : "My hour is come, I have reached the goal. Has it not been worth a struggle of some thirty years down here, to win ages of immortal glory ?"

Her tired eyes now closed, and she entered upon the final conflict. That was a moment of strange and holy significance to all of us. At this time of utter helplessness, when we had come to feel that any power which might raise her would be simply miraculous, a great inexpressible sighing, or rather, a groaning which no words could utter, ascended up to God from out of the hearts gathered round that lowly bed.

Suddenly our father roused himself, as if from a dream, and signing to the children to follow, left the chamber of mourning. Inquiring looks accompanied the band on their way upstairs, the little ones thronging like sheep behind a shepherd, not knowing whither they went. Quickly opening his study door, the father marshalled them round the table, and bade them kneel, himself taking the central place. Then, drawing off the customary little velvet cap from his head, and with folded hands, he prayed that, although he did not deserve the mercy, God would take pity upon him and his children, and leave them the mother whom they so sorely needed. Down upon our knees, we children felt a mysterious thrill pass through us. It seemed as if we had been admitted within the upper sanctuary, before the throne of the Everlasting God. A vivid expectancy had taken the place of tears, when, with a glance of deep tenderness, our father said: "Now, children, let us go back." And out we stepped again in his wake, down into the silent chamber where many still stood waiting, and as we entered, they looked up at us wonderingly, as if they would have asked whether we had gotten a glimpse into the high places of Him, whose seat is above the clouds, in whose hands are poised the mystic balances that weigh out life and death.

Again we resumed our posts of watching, but who can picture what was going on within our hearts, for into them had entered a calm, deep and still, like the calm of eternity. No movement or grief was visible now; all the company seemed to be holding their breath. Only our eyes were active still, and they remained fixed upon that colorless face on the pillow—and fixed indeed with such intensity, as if our gaze could draw her back to this life of ours.

It was not long before, suddenly opening her eyes—already closed, as it seemed, in the death-sleep—she spoke, almost inaudibly: "Let the people all go. I shall not die."

The room was noiselessly emptied of its

occupants, and from that hour, she gradually began to recover. Before long, she related the following incidents. "I stood at the very door of eternity, and saw my brothers who had come to fetch me and was rejoicing greatly at the thought of our eternal union. All at once it occurred to me that if my life on earth could be of further service to my children, I wished God might restore it, and immediately it was impressed upon me that He would do so."

The illness lasted eleven weeks longer, but we felt happy all the time, in the quiet confidence that God had given our beloved mother back to us. What He had given us in her, and with her, we little thought: the future was to reveal it.

CHAPTER II.

The Lads.

According to the normal order of things, a man finds his course in life marked out for him among public and professional duties, while the sphere of women is limited to domestic occupations, and the care and training of families. Now-a-days this system is overturned in many cases, where, as the saying goes, "the man cooks, and the wife dictates;" but in our house the ancient fashion prevailed in full force, and my father in no wise troubled himself as to the internal economy or the children's education; all these matters lay exclusively under our mother's jurisdiction, so much so, indeed, that with our grandmother's help, she was obliged even to give the lads the grounding of their classical education. It was well for us that circumstances had fitted her for the post of teacher. In her youth our grandmother had studied with her father's pupils, until she could have passed the University entrance-examination with greater ease than any of them; and as our mother's education had been equally thorough, she was quite at home among both Greek and Latin classics.

Only that, being obliged at the same time to conduct the household arrangements of a large family, the methods of teaching she was often forced to adopt differed so widely from those of a well-ordered school, that a professional pedagogue might have wrung his hands in horror at witnessing them. It would sometimes happen, for instance, that while she stood busily engaged at the washing tub, we boys formed a circle round her, and jumping up and down in measured steps, recited, or rather sang, through the Latin declensions. She could seldom find quiet time for Bible history lessons in the day, so that this branch of study was mostly postponed until we lay in our beds in the evening. Then, sitting beside us, she would picture Bible scenes in such vivid colors that we were completely fascinated. When she did not appear quickly on these occasions we used to lie waiting in the greatest impatience, crying in a shrill key from time to time, "Mother, come tell us, tell us!" When very tired, she occasionally herself lay down to rest while narrating: but if she showed any symptoms of falling asleep and ceasing her tales, the young voices roused her with the ever-recurring question: "What then, mother?"

Once, feeling worn out, she was thus resting, while recounting the conversation of Jesus with Nicodemus, and every moment seemed on the point of dropping off into slumber, so that the chorus of our voices sounded incessantly in urging her on. At length, quite overcome with drowsiness, she made one strong final effort to rouse her drooping faculties, and took up our question : " And then, the Saviour said " O Nicodemus ! you might just as well have come in the daytime."

At which assertion, we became aware that it was best to give up our delightful story for the time being, and let her rest in peace.

These lessons went on for some time, but she soon saw that it would be impossible for our education to flourish under such circumstances, and that we must be put into a proper school if we were to get forward in earnest. Our father, looking upon his very narrow means, would not hear of such a thing, and gave it as his opinion that an honest shoemaker was better off than a poor parson, and that unless one had means to educate the lads, it was much best to put them to a respectable trade.

Our mother, however, could not see the force of these arguments, and finally resolved to place her sons at school, trusting that God would help her to provide funds to carry them through a regular course of study. The two eldest, aged eleven and twelve, were thus dispatched to Leonberg, where, through the influence of a friend, who was glad to make some return for kindness she had once shown him, they gained admittance into a good and cheap boarding-house. Our father, however, refused to contribute anything towards the expense incurred, and though only a small sum was required, the responsibility of providing it weighed heavily upon our mother. She could only obtain it by selling the produce of some fields attached to the parsonage, the management of which had always been left entirely to her care. Now, therefore, she made it her great object skilfully to husband these resources. She rarely hired laborers, but did the chief part of the field work herself, with the help of her daughters. At the same time, whilst continuing to supply the table as usual for my father, she and the children ate their frugal meals with the servants, their unvarying bill of fare being soup for breakfast, vegetables and dumplings for dinner, and sour milk with potatoes for supper. Meat was a luxury produced only on Sundays, and rare occasions. By means of such severe economy, she actually succeeded in supplying the requisite funds, though not always quite regularly. Now and then, blight, drought, or other trials of that sort disturbed the order of things: then distress prevailed, and good counsel would have been precious had we known where to go for it.

On one occasion, shortly before harvest, the fields stood thick with corn, and our mother had already calculated that their produce would suffice to meet all claims for the year. She was standing at the window casting the matter over in her mind, with great satisfaction, when her attention was suddenly caught by some heavy black clouds with white borders, drifting at a great rate across the summer sky. "It is a hailstorm!" she exclaimed in dismay, and quickly throwing up the window, she leaned out. Her eyes rested upon a frightful mass of wild storm cloud, covering the western horizon and approaching with rapid fury.

"O God!" she cried, "there comes an awful tempest, and what *is* to become of my corn!" The black masses rolled nearer and nearer, while the ominous rushing movement that precedes a storm began to rock the sultry air, and the dreaded hailstorms fell with violence. Half beside herself with anxiety about those fields lying at the eastern end of the valley, she now lifted her hands heavenward, and wringing them in terror cried, "Dear Father in heaven, what art Thou doing? Thou knowest I cannot manage to pay for my boys at school, without the produce of those fields! Oh! turn Thy hand, and do not let the hail blast my hopes!" Scarcely, however, had these words crossed her lips when she started, for it seemed to her as if a voice had whispered in her ear, "Is my arm shortened that it cannot help thee in other ways?" Abashed, she shrank into a quiet corner, and there entreated God to forgive her want of faith. In the meantime the storm passed. And now various neighbors hurried in, proclaiming that the whole valley lay thickly covered with hailstones, down to the very edge of the parsonage fields, but the latter had been quite spared. The storm had reached their border, and then suddenly taken another direction into the next valley. Moreover, that the whole village was in amazement, declaring that God had wrought a miracle for the sake of our mother whom He loved. She listened, silently adoring the goodness of the Lord, and vowing that henceforth her confidence should be only in Him.

CHAPTER III.

The Place Above the Trap-Door.

There is a story of a famous astronomer who once predicted fine weather for a particular day on which he invited some guests to a garden party. When they had assembled, it began to rain, and his friends remarking upon the failure of his expectations, he rejoined: "I may make an almanac, but our Lord God makes the weather." We could all tell instances of the differing in our Heavenly Father's ways from ours, as testified by an old adage, "None can climb into God's cabinet." At times the variation between His plans and ours is so startling, that His ways proclaim themselves as not only wonderful, but "past finding out."

Five of my mother's six boys had by this time been placed in different schools, and it may be imagined that the task of providing for them almost out-stripped her power. Thus it came to pass one year that the demands for the various payments had been several times repeated. The burden of care was of itself enough for our mother, but it became intolerable when accompanied by the incessant reproaches of her husband, who would say, "There, you see! I always told you that you were attempting impossible things. You would take your own way, sending out one lad after another, and now your self-will is going to bring disgrace upon us."

In the face of this accusation, our mother boldly stood by her assertion that God would never leave her in trouble, and she expected

Him to help very soon. These discussions always ended by our father giving way with the words, "Well, we shall see, *tempus doucebit!*" (time will show!)

Things were in this uncomfortable state, when, as he was one day sitting alone in his study, lost in thought, a knock at the door announced the entrance of the postman, bringing three letters from the different towns where the boys were boarding. Each of them contained the same message, which was, that unless the dues could be settled at once, the lads would be dismissed. Our father read the letters with growing excitement, and spread them out upon the table to show his wife, who had hardly crossed the threshold when he cried, "There, look at them and pay our debts with your faith! I have no money nor can I tell where to go for any."

Seizing the papers, she rapidly glanced through them with a very grave face, but then answered firmly, "It is all right: the business shall be settled. For He who says, 'The gold and silver is mine,' will find it an easy thing to provide these sums." Saying which, she hastily left the room.

Our father readily supposed she intended making her way to a certain rich friend who had helped us before. He was mistaken, for this time her steps turned in a different direction. We had in the parsonage an upper loft, shut off by a trap-door from the lower one, and over this door it was that she now knelt down and began to deal with Him in whose strength she had undertaken the work of her children's education. She spread before Him those letters from the study table, and told Him of her husband's half scoffing taunt. She also reminded Him how her life had been redeemed from the very gates of death, for the children's sake, and then declared that she could not believe that He meant to forsake her at this juncture; she was willing to be the *second* whom He might forsake, but she was determined not to be the *first*.

In the meanwhile, her husband waited downstairs, and night came on; but she did not appear. Supper was ready, and yet she stayed in the loft. Then the eldest girl, her namesake Beatè, ran up to call her; but the answer was: "Take your supper without me, it is not time for me to eat." Late in the evening, the little messenger was again despatched, but returned with the reply, "Go to bed; the time has not come for me to rest." A third time, at breakfast next morning, the girl called her mother.

"Leave me alone," she said; "I do not need breakfast, when I am ready I shall come." Thus the hours sped on, and downstairs her husband and the children began to feel frightened, not daring however to disturb her any more. At last the door opened, and she entered, her face beaming with a wonderful light. The little daughter thought that something extraordinary must have happened; and running to her mother with open arms, asked eagerly, "What is it? Did an angel from heaven bring the money?" "No, my child," was the smiling answer, "but now I am sure that it will come." She had hardly spoken, when a maid in peasant costume entered, saying: "The master of the Linden Inn sends to ask whether the Frau Pastorin can spare the time to see him?" "Ah, I know what he wants," answered our mother. "My best regards, and I will come at once." Whereupon she started, and mine host, looking out of his window, saw her from afar, and came forward to welcome her with the words, "O Madame, how glad I am you have come!" Then leading her into his back parlor he said: "I cannot tell how it is, but the whole of this last night I could not sleep for thinking of you. For some time I have had several hundred *gulden* lying in that chest, and all night long I was haunted by the thought that you needed this money, and that I ought to give it to you. If that be the case, there it is—take it. And do not trouble about repaying me. Should you be able to make it up again, well and good—if not, never mind." On this my mother said: "Yes, I do most certainly need it, my kind friend; for all last night I too was awake, crying to God for help. Yesterday there came three letters, telling us that all our boys would be dismissed unless the money for their board is cleared at once."

"Is it really so?" exclaimed the innkeeper, who was a noble-hearted and spiritual Christian man. "How strange and wonderful! Now I am doubly glad I asked you to come!" Then opening the chest, he produced three weighty packets, and handed them to her with a prayer that God's blessing might rest upon the gift. She accepted it with the simple words, "May God make good to you this service of Christian sympathy. For you have acted as the steward of One who has promised not even to leave the giving of a cup of cold water unrewarded."

Husband and children were eagerly awaiting her at home, and those three dismal letters still lay open on the table, when the mother, who had quitted that study in such deep emotion the day before, stepped up to her husband radiant with joy. On each letter, she laid a roll of money and then cried, " Look, there it is! And now believe that faith in God is no empty madness!"

CHAPTER IV.

Every-day Life.

Before continuing a series of instances which show how God honored the firm though humble faith of this gifted woman, a slight sketch of her every-day life will not fail to interest our readers : we resume the narrative of her son.

As, except on rare occasions, our father left the whole task of family discipline to our mother's care, she often found difficulty in rendering herself mistress of the responsible position she was forced to occupy, especially as, far from being model children, we boys were high spirited, mischievous urchins. According to her usual plan, however, she committed all her ways to the Lord ; and then, instead of desponding at the thought of all she could *not* do, set cheerily to work, determined to perform faithfully whatever lay in her power.

Her first principle in education was, to establish a marked distinction between mere failings and actual sins; and while we were promptly reproved and even punished for disorder, heedlessness, or unpunctuality, it was done in the way of discipline. But whenever an instance of deceit, ingratitude, or unkindness came to light, the whole character of her dealing was altered. It seemed to us that she then assumed the attitude of God's priests or prophets of the olden time. Deep solemnity accompanied her words, so that, as she represented the heinous nature of our offence, we felt them pierce our very joints and marrow, conveying such a terrible sense of guilt that we hardly knew how to bear it, and would have preferred ten beatings to one such " sermon," as we called it. A strong influence was exerted by her plan of telling us Bible stories at night. We looked forward with longing to these delightful hours, and listened entranced to her vivid pictures; which resulted in giving us an intimate acquaintance with Scripture, so that in subsequent public examinations, I, for my part, distanced all competitors in this branch, and astonished the examiners themselves.

But the most mighty secret power she gained over us was by the force of a holy life. We could not help seeing how free it was from all wordly principle; vanity, self indulgence or avarice. So simple and frugal were her personal habit, that even in after-years, when we tried to persuade her, for the sake of health, to take more care of herself, the invariable reply would be, "Leave me the food and clothes I am used to: they will do well enough for this world. All the ease I might enjoy here would fail to satisfy me in the end. There would always be something wanting still. So I will be content and wait till I get over yonder, where we shall wear garments which will never grow old, and our hunger and thirst will be satisfied forever."

Daily we saw her gaze directed above, to the things which are unfading and celestial. Her one aim was to sacrifice herself in order to serve others, and to act for eternity. All the striking proofs of blessing, strewn like stars across the dark night of her earthly struggle, show how God owned this singleness of purpose.

No sooner were we, lads, away from home, than, instead of joining the ranks of the steady and orderly, we made common cause with the most mischievous and daring among our schoolfellows; and it might have seemed as if all home-training had gone for nothing. But the seed so deeply sown in our hearts was only buried, not lost, and at last maintained its principle of life, in the face of adverse influences. At the age of fifteen, I was at the Seminary of Maulbronn, belonging to the most merry fun-loving set of boys there, when one day, there arose amongst us a great talk about pietism, some arguing in its favor, and others against it. At last, I spoke out boldly and said, "I don't know much about it, but they say my mother is a pietist. If that is true, and if the others are like her, I can only say pietism is *real* goodness, and the straight way to heaven. After what I have seen and gone through at home, I am so sure of this, that I shall never be able to doubt the reality of it." "Well then," rejoined a schoolfellow, "why ever are you what you are? Why don't you set up for a pietist yourself, without more ado?"

"You are right," I answered, "but you see what has not happened yet may come to pass some day: and it shall, too!"

Some years later, several of us were visiting our uncle, a rationalist professor at Heidelberg. Knowing our mother's principles, he was anxious to find out how far they had taken root in our minds, and often tried to perplex us with religious inquiries.

Sister Beatè was the grand champion of our party. He would ask her, "Come now, tell me, what do you take God to be? Is not God the universal principle of Goodness?" "No," she promptly answered; "God is *the good One*"—(not a vague principle, but a Person). My brother, who was studying medicine, he advised to direct his attention to the secrets of nature, which, he declared, would solve the mystery of many miracles. He surmised it would be very possible to discover some subtile tincture which might impart to water the color and flavor of wine, and such means had probably been used by our Lord at the marriage feast of Cana.

"No indeed," my brother answered sturdily, "such tinctures are not to be found here among men; they are above in the hand of Him who created the whole world out of nothing."

At length, laying by his weapons, our uncle was fain to confess, "Well, after all, you are your mother's own children."

A few years later, suddenly, as in the spring

time, the seed that had long lain sleeping in our hearts, having taken root, sprang up vigorously. Before the eldest of us had left the University, we had each and all made a free and individual choice, to walk with our mother in the narrow way which leads to life eternal.

One of her most common practices in daily life was, to direct our attention to the parables God has laid up for us in His wonderful book of Nature. In the garden, the field and the house, she reminded us in a few simple words of these lessons. The weeds, the green trees, the blights on our plants, as well as our daily tasks and interests, were all examined, and the hidden meaning and type in each clearly noted, with a freshness and originality that worked them forcibly upon our memories. Sometimes, without any seeming reason, she would tell us many of the wise, happy thoughts with which her mind seemed to overflow; it was the lips running over out of "the fulness of the heart."

Coming home one day from an expedition in which she had vainly attempted to borrow a sum of money for the pressing claims of her sons' education, Beatè met her, and imagined from her cheerful looks that the money had been forthcoming, for she had left home sad and downcast. "No," said she, "but God has comforted me. As I turned away sorrowfully, after having been refused, I felt so weak and wretched, that I could hardly walk. All at once, there came into my mind that verse in the story of Abraham and Isaac: "And they went, both of them together." Then I thought; these words were not put into the Bible without a reason, especially as they are repeated twice:

Genesis XXII; 6, 8. God saw what was passing in the heart of Abraham as he climbed that mountain with his son. And indeed it is evident that Abraham's distress had then reached the highest pitch. He was to sacrifice the life of his only son. With me, the question relates not to the temporal, but to the spiritual life of my six boys; for that will be endangered if their studies are given up. But now I am sure God sees, and has noted it in His book; and this conforts me."

The sense of consolation was so lively and strong within her, that for weeks after, she called the attentien of everyone she met to this passage, adding, "Thus we often have to go a weary pilgrimage, but God sees it. He knows how our hearts are feeling, and writes it in His book." Another time she had a letter from a beloved and honored uncle, in which he reproached her bitterly for persisting in the education of the boys, when she had not sufficient means to carry it out. This grieved her so deeply, that she became quite ill, took to her bed, and could do nothing but weep. Her daughter wondered to see her so unnerved, because, in a general way, she troubled herself little as to other people's opinions, and often used to say, "Never mind, I can wait until God justifies me." Now however, she exclaimed: "If it only had been some one else I should not care. But this uncle is just the one friend I need, and who has always stood by me till now!" No comfort seemed to find its way to her heart, till the next morning, when, rising again calm and happy, she told Beatè, "I have examined myself as to whether there is any truth in what they say—that pride and self-will have been actuating me, but it is not so. My reason for persevering with the boys is the good of their souls. All persons, especially young ones, must have some ruling interest and enjoyment in life. If our lads cannot pursue the studies they care for, they will soon find out other pleasures, those of sense; and such will quickly lead them into sin. Besides, now I see them twice a year, and am able to exert a strong influence over them still, whereas, if they left home to learn a trade, they would be taken quite out of my reach. Then again, I should be positively ashamed to meet my father in heaven, unless I had done everything in my power to raise and ennoble my children, both in body and soul. He denied himself so sternly in order to bring us up to a good standing; and how could

I look into his face with joy if I had failed in forwarding the best interests of his grand-children? I know I am justified before God, so now I can feel quiet, for the Bible says, "If a man's ways please the Lord, He maketh even His enemies to be at peace with him."

Scarcely ten years had gone by, before all her friends, and this uncle most especially, were ready to own and honor the triumph of her faith, so that she could remind them of this occasion with the words: "Did I not say so? God keeps all his promises. Every jot and tittle is fulfilled to those whose ways please Him."

Little time had she for reading, even the Bible; and yet although perfectly simple and unaffected in her discourse, which was peculiarly free from religious phrasealogy, her daily life was a clear and constant witness against worldliness of form or practice. Each morning she awoke with some text or holy verse upon her mind, and this she appointed as a subject and motto for the day, and it furnished her with light, strength and spiritual food.

Once in going a journey, instead of taking the comfortable place behind, she insisted on sitting in front of the small conveyance in which a farmer was driving her. Years afterwards the man would speak of that drive and the long talk that lasted through it. "It was the most delightful journey I ever went in my life," said the honest fellow, a firm friend of my mother; "it was a distance of thirty-six miles, but the time passed like nothing, and I could hardly believe my eyes when we reached the end." It was her daily verse that furnished the whole topic of this conversation.

CHAPTER V.

King William.

By the time our father had held the Living of Thalheim nearly ten years, and we were in the midst of our school career, a letter from the Royal Consistory was one day brought to our house, and plunged both our parents into deep anxiety. At the time of his presentation to the Living, it had been considered too valuable for a man of his age, and the Consistory therefore requested him to contribute annually a certain portion of the stipend towards a fund for the amelioration of poorer livings. On the plea of his large family he petitioned against this order, and receiving no reply or further official application, he concluded that the matter had been decided in his favor. And now, after all these years, the whole arrears were suddenly claimed, with a sharp reprimand for past neglect of payment. On the ground of recent losses through hail, our father excused himself from immediate compliance, and obtained a remission of half the debt. But a year's respite soon passed by, and a crisis of care and distress approached. Day by day our mother grew more oppressed as the term of payment drew on apace. Just then we received a visit from a clergyman, an intimate friend, who, struck by our mother's evident and unusual sadness, ventured to ask its cause. She told him her tale of care, and he at once saw well that any further petition on our father's part would be quite out of place. At the same time he advised her to apply, not to the council, but direct to the King himself, who was known and beloved as a true father of his country, with an open ear for all that were oppressed. Between them, our friend and herself, they at once composed a letter fully stating the facts of the case, together with all circumstances calculated to work upon the sympathies of a feeling heart. This petition was despatched to a cousin of our mother's, then in attendance upon the young Crown Prince, with a request that it might be presented, if possible, with a word of recommendation. At the time the letter reached the palace the little prince lay ill, and his disease was taking a dangerous type, so that the good cousin hardly knew how to proceed, and for some time carried the papers about, waiting for a favorable moment. One day, as she was watching by the bed of the royal child, the King and Queen came in to visit him. The little fellow, lying weak and ill in his cot, stretched out his hands with joy at the sight of his father, who gently clasped the boy and drew him to his heart. In the mean time our cousin handed the papers to the Queen, who, glancing them over and becoming interested and touched, handed them to her husband. He scanned the writing, and then read the whole attentively, after which, taking out a pencil, he wrote underneath: "I undertake to defray the whole debt out of my private purse." At the same time he ordered this message to be sent by express-post to the pastor's wife at Thalheim.

Night had come on by the time the royal courier reached Tuttlingen, our nearest town; but according to the strict order a postilion mounted immediately to carry the dispatch to its destination. Day had not broken, when he came galloping up our village street, blowing from his post-horn a blast so shrill and clear, that all the good neighbors awoke, stretched their heads out of their respective windows, and asked what could be the matter. At length, the clattering horse hoofs drew up beneath the parsonage walls. Our mother was up and ready to hear the errand of the postilion, who handed over his message; and hastening back into the house, she read the cheering answer to her prayer. With folded hands and tears of joy she cried, "Verily, Thou art a God that hidest Thyself. One day, an innkeeper is Thy paymaster, and another a king, by the grace of God! Oh! repay our Sovereign for this his goodness to us, and bless him in soul and body, in time and eternity, Thou King of kings! Amen."

CHAPTER VI.

The Neighbors, and Our Mother's Work Amongst Them.

The scene of our mother's most prolonged activity was the before-mentioned village of Thalheim, lying in a narrow valley of a district commonly called the "Baar," part of the mountainous Black Forest. Its inhabitants are distinguished by peculiarities both of costume and character. Their strong and handsome physical development is united to the free simple manners, and marked individualities of race, only observable among Highlanders. The power of custom exercises a singular force over the minds and actions of these primitive folks; it may indeed be described as the strongest moral or spiritual influence in the whole region. In their eyes it would seem an enormity to make light of their traditional notions of propriety, and the mighty law of "custom" is incongruously dragged forward upon all occasions, often even to pronounce upon matters of the most serious nature.

Once, in remonstrating with a naughty maid, my mother asked her how, in following her evil courses she could ever expect to get to heaven. "Why not, I should like to know?" cried the girl in surprise. "Upon what do you found your hopes?" asked my mother. "O Frau Pastorin!" rejoined the damsel with much assurance, "it is the *custom* with us for people to go to heaven! You see, heaven was made for us—not for the animals."

The dialect of the Baar is harsh and odd,

somewhat resembling the Swiss patois, and possessing a quaint force and drollery of its own. The costume of the place is still more singular, and might seem almost to date back to primeval ages.

A woman's head-gear consists of two caps, one black and tight fitting, drawn down in front to meet the eyebrows, the other of fur, which is worn the whole year round. Two long plaits of hair hang down the back reaching far toward the ground. A black jacket, drawn back in front, exposes a laced vest surmounted by white. Round the waist is passed a thick sausage-shaped roll, from under which emerges the skirt, starched stiffly into innumerable tiny folds. Broad, flat shoes, and red woolen hose, complete this strange attire, which altogether weighs twenty pounds, and costs from fifteen to twenty dollars. The wedding costume (or "hippé," as it is called) generally lasts a woman her life time. A very curious effect is produced in the village church, by the sight of the whole female population, down to the smallest girl, dressed in this way, and ranged in long rows. Without this traditional costume however, none of them would set foot within a place of worship.

On one occasion, my mother went round the whole village, vainly trying to hunt up such a dress for a poor unthriftly woman, who had confessed to her with shame and contrition, that she dared not show herself, for want of a "hippé." In every house she was met by the contemptuous reply, "If she were not a lazy wench, she would have her dress all right enough!" At length, in the cottage of a charcoal burner, the guest proved successful, for his wife, though very poor, immediately discovered that she possessed an extra "hippé," which she freely offered. Deeply touched by this general kindness, and in the name of Him who said, "I was naked, and ye clothed me," our mother accepted the gift. She also formed a very hearty friendship with the charcoal owner's wife, who was a most interesting woman, endowed with mental capacity and refinement of a high order, while her disposition was frank and affectionate. Her active kindness and sympathy often proved a real comfort to us.

It was on the New Year's Eve of 1820 that, as our mother sat reviewing her past life, it occurred to her that the store of her father's sermons, hitherto read alone, might be made a means of wide-spread blessing, if a few of the neighbors were to assemble and listen to them in the parlor of her above-mentioned friend. The plan was promptly adopted, and henceforth a company of peasant women met regularly and found great enjoyment in hearing them. The spiritual life of the charcoal-burner's wife especially seemed to receive a marked impulse, so that our mother exclaimed in delight, "One actually sees her grow!" The good woman, on her part, seemed to become more glad-hearted every day, as she sat mending the garments of her large family during the reading; and often declared, "It is only since 'the mother'* came among us that I have found out what I really am and possess; the more I get to know God's word, the more I hunger and thirst after it." Her cordial affection to our mother increased in

* Throughout the whole village Madame Paulus was always called "the mother."

the meantime, and if ever she noticed the parsonage lights burning late at night, she would come running over and say, "I don't know how it is, Madam, but I cannot sleep when you are up and busy!" And then, actively taking part in any business that was on hand, she stayed on till all was finished.

Some years later this faithful woman died in my mother's arms; and often, in speaking of her, she used to assure us that in "the resurrection of the just" the charcoal-burner's wife would be distinguished and honored as the model of a Christian neighbor.

On leaving home, the ancient Greek colonists were always supplied with holy fire from their country's hearth, in order to keep up the glow of patriotism in their hearts, and show their connection with their native land. Surely, we ought, in the same way, to supply our children, those colonists whom we send out into the far country of the Future, with a holy flame of truth and light, such as is furnished for us in the Word of God. This was an idea which forced itself very strongly upon our mother's mind, and caused her to adopt a plan originated by our grandmother. It consisted in assembling the village children, and by the aid of a large colored picture-book, relating Scripture stories to them in a lively and impressive manner. Every Sunday afternoon, she started out, the book under her arm, and going from house to house, gathered round her everywhere a crowd of eager listeners. When she quitted one cottage, the children, intent on hearing more of her attractive stories, ran along by her side into the next. It was a curious sight, this wandering

Sunday-school, such as has rarely been seen, the shepherd in the midst of the flock, the crook being replaced by the famous picture-book, her sign of office; and as she passed up the street, her narrative was often continued for the benefit of apt scholars. This method of teaching embraced one grand advantage, inasmuch as each visit gave opportunities of hearing the truth, to the grown up as well as to the younger members of every family, and many a good seed was thus cast by the wayside. We can see here how ingenious in its resources is the love that seeks and saves.*

But our mother's most practical and efficient

* Sunday-schools were at this time an unknown institution in Germany. They were introduced into Stuttgart about eight years ago, by a German who returned home for a visit, after being many years in America. They soon took root, and are now universal throughout that city, and are conducted on the American plan.

labor was one unseen by others, for it was accomplished when all around her were at rest. By the time night had set in, and her daily household toil was ended, her great night work began. For then, she entered into communion with a higher world, and like Jacob, wrestled with God in prayer, for special blessings upon her family and friends, our parish and all her other interests. This was done with so much constancy and regularity, that at least two nights in each week were thus spent. When, in later days, we begged that she would allow herself more rest, she always said, "I shall rest in eternity, *now* I have no time. I have to pray so much for the king, and government, the consistory, universities, seminaries, and schools, beside my own family, that I seem never to have finished." Her cabinet of business for this spiritual work, was a little corner beside the stove in her room, and there she spent countless nights kneeling or stretched upon the floor, yet never growing weary.

CHAPTER VII.

The Broken Home.

It is one thing, when a ship is tossing on mid-ocean, and has all sorts of shoals, quicksands, and tempests before it; but it is quite another, when most of the weary way lies behind, and the shores of the country whither it is bound begin to loom in view. This was the state of things in our house ten years after our mother began her task of educating us. Two of the elder ones were already at college, while another was supporting himself by his profession, and contributing part of his earnings to help the younger members.

Our father had at length reconciled himself to the order of things, and delighted in showing off the attainments of his three tall lads among our friendly neighbors. It gratified him for people to notice the very apparent signs of chemical industry on William's "working hands," as he always called them; and whenever Philip, the theologian, came home, he had to preach, catechise, and visit; while Fritz, the medical student, tried his hand at writing prescriptions of medicine, which was to cure the various ailments of the sick villagers. Not our father alone, but all the people of the neighborhood sympathized in our enterprises, and rejoiced at our culture and progress; for everyone knew that the pastor had no private property, and the fact of his sons receiving professional educations was a puzzle to many.

Once a kind professor expressed his surprise to me upon this point. So I told him our secret, which was that our mother, who managed the whole affair, had the help and support of some one who bears the wonderful key which fits and opens all the cash boxes of earth. But although our poor mother had struggled through many difficulties and sorrows, the worst still awaited her. The experiences of life had greatly altered my father's opinions, and instead of holding his former rationalistic views, he now owned a lively Christian faith. About this time the presentiment of his approaching removal to a higher life seemed forcibly impressed on his mind, so that one day, calling his daughter to him, he said: "Beatè, my time for remaining with you is short. I shall be suddenly struck by the hand of death, and I wish you to promise that when you see me lying at the last extremity you will whisper in my ear the name of Jesus; for I want to go through the dark valley carrying that name within my soul."

The child gave her word, little thinking how soon she would be called upon to fulfil it. Very shortly our father sickened, and at once sank into such weakness that all were greatly alarmed, and before his absent children could be summoned, he died. When Beatè whispered the Savior's name in his ear, during the last moments, his glaring eyes once more lighted up in grateful love, and then closed forever.

A large concourse of friends met to celebrate the funeral, among them many neighboring clergymen. One of these had dreaded meeting our mother, for he thought that the ruins of all her hopes, in this sudden stroke, would have crushed her into despair. Throughout the mournful service he watched her closely, but to his surprise she appeared calm and at rest. At the close, he could not refrain from expressing his wonder. "What does it mean?" he asked; "all the plans and the joy of your life are swept away, and yet you are composed and cheerful!"

"Ah, dear friend," she replied, with a beaming face, "I certainly was almost distracted as I started to walk into that sad procession to-day, with my nine orphan children; especially when we stood in church, and I looked upon the coffin with which all my hopes for this life were to be buried. At that moment it was midnight in my soul; I saw no star in heaven, and no path on earth. Then I lifted my eyes unto Him who, up to this time, had been my only hope and refuge, and begged for one beam of His eternal love to shine into my beclouded heart. Suddenly it was as if a voice cried in my ear:

'Be still and take no care. Henceforth God alone will provide for you and your children! It shall be just as it was when He took Moses away, and the children of Israel had scarcely reached the borders of the promised land. He saw fit to bring His people into Canaan without the help of their old leader, so that everyone might see it was all His work.'

"In listening to these words my heart grew light, and I answered, 'If that is so, I am content, and even the dark path shall be a joyful way to me!' It is this that strengthens me. For I know He is faithful, and keeps all His promises."

CHAPTER VIII.

The New House, and Our First Vacation There.

"Our faithful Lord has taken the rudder of your little craft into His own hands, and He will pilot it on safely to the haven." It was with this conviction firmly fastened in her heart that our mother entered the narrow path of widowhood. However, she knew little of the trials and lessons which awaited her in it.

The last days of our life in the old homestead at Thalheim were hastening to a close, and there was barely time to put matters into the order necessitated by altered circumstances.

Our mother's future dwelling was to be in the house of a widowed aunt at Münchingen, where a humble lodging had been offered her, and although it seemed scarcely possible to find space for herself and four children in the two or three little rooms placed at her disposal, still, in the absence of pecuniary means, she gratefully took advantage of our relative's kindness.

The expenses of removal exceeded her calculations, and left her in possession of a few *gulden* only. It was thus necessary to save every farthing, and she therefore decided to *walk* nine miles of the journey. The last night was watched through at the parsonage, now bare of all furniture, and a few sympathizing friends shared our vigil. At three in the morning we were to start, but before that time such heavy rain began, that we almost despaired of being able to walk; and yet a post-chaise awaited us, nine miles off, at six in the morning.

Just at this juncture, a ponderous double-teamed waggon rumbled up the wood, and halted at our door. It belonged to a peasant, who had intended driving a load of corn to some distance, but seeing the rain, had postponed his business, to be able to offer us his services, "so that no one might ever say that the villagers of Thalheim had let their pastor's widow walk out of their town in such a drenching storm of rain. Our party safely reached their new abode, having half way overtaken the carrier in charge of our furniture, who had, oddly enough, forgotten where he was to take it, and was asking all the people along the road whether they could tell him.

Our arrangements in the new quarters were the *nec plus ultra* of simplicity, yet the whole party soon came to feel happy, in spite of inconveniences. Not only our aunt and the landlord, who lived on respective flats of the same house, but the whole village beside, seemed intent on showing kindness to the grand-daughter of their former beloved pastor, Flattich. In truth, they had always done the same, for when, as children, they visited at Münchingen, the rich peasants used to insist on giving us presents, and often accompanied us miles on our homeward way, carrying our knapsacks. Indeed some years before, when I had entered the Seminary at Maulbronn, the wife of a farmer at Münchingen sent an order to an acquaintance living near me to furnish me with a large bowl of bread and milk every morning, at her expense. I did not know whence this daily meal fell to my share, but it caused great satisfaction to me and the various friends who helped me despatch it. This is only one instance of the affection of these peasants for the memory of their old pastor, after a lapse of forty years from his death. Indeed to this day, the mention of his name quickens the beat of those warm faithful hearts.

Soon after the arrival at Münchingen, three of the boys came home for their vacation. The small parlor scarcely sufficed to hold us all, but the great joy of being together again was not disturbed by the narrow limits of our dwelling. A fresh trouble, however, and one which could not be so easily put aside, now made itself felt. Our funds had come to an end, and the store of household provisions melted away perceptibly, so that one evening there was nothing for it, but for us to go fasting to bed. This was too much for our mother, and she said: "Am I to have my children here, and not even be able to give them food? God cannot mean this to be so!" And without more ado, she threw herself on the ground beside the stove, and wrestled in earnest prayer the whole night through, and when we entered the next morning there she still lay. We tried to raise her, and said: "Dear mother, let us breakfast. Even if there is not earthly food provided, we still have the bread which is come down from heaven, the Word of God. We will gather round that and enjoy it." But our words availed nothing; she still lay, while we, seating ourselves, opened our Bibles, read, sang, and prayed.

Hardly had we said Amen, when a well dressed, veiled lady entered, after knocking, and begged to speak to our sister in private. Beatè led her to an attic, apologizing for having no other place of reception. And then the lady, the widow of a professor from the neighboring village of Kornthal, explained herself thus:

"I cannot think what has come over me this morning. I woke at six o'clock with these words in my ear, 'Get up, and take something out of your purse to Madame Paulus, at Münchingen.' I demurred, never having heard that she was in need of money: but the same impression repeated itself upon my mind continually, and each time in a more lively manner, until at last, in despair of getting any peace, I yielded. So I come, begging you to accept this sum, although I do not know whether you want it or not." With grateful joy, Beatè took the little packet of coin, and after our visitor had gone, came down, triumphantly holding it in her hand, whilst she cried, "Now, mother, rise! Our distress is over. God has sent a widow from Kornthal to bring you this help."

CHAPTER IX.

The Rent.

It is well known that the human heart is something like a stringed instrument, with a wonderful variety of chords, some deep, harsh, and powerful, others quite tremulous and delicate.

In the feminine temperament, the latter are occasionally developed to an extent almost incredible, and quite unattainable to the other sex. One of these tender chords in my mother's disposition was that of gratitude. If a way of showing her warm appreciation of a kindness could possibly be devised, no pains or exertion in carrying it out were taken into account. Thus, when I first went to school, we had a cousin, who, on finding that I could not be lodged in the preceptor's house, took me into his own, and always treated me with the greatest kindness. Some years after, he became a candidate for a civil post, and begged us to use our influence on his behalf. Straightway our mother left all her own work, and starting out called on all the voters of the neighborhood, not resting until she had secured their support for our friend, who gained the appointment in consequence of these vigorous exertions. The delicacy of our mother's gratitude was peculiarly manifested toward our kind aunt, who, at the cost of much self-denial, had made room for our party in her house. The trifling rent due for our rooms was rigorously put by and paid to the day; for our relative, as we well knew, had only enough property to render her barely independent.

Once more our vacation came around, and we all were united at home. This time food was forthcoming, but on the other hand, the approaching rent-day weighed heavily on our family purse—light as ever—and on my poor mother's mind. Each day she grew more heavy-hearted, often saying that the money *must* be paid in time, for she knew our aunt depended on it.

The term had actually arrived when she gathered us round her one morning, saying, "Come, let us ask God to step into the midst of us and take this matter into His own hands." She then uttered this prayer: "Faithful Savior, Thou knowest this is the rent-day. Once when Thou didst need tribute money, a fish out of the sea was sent to bring it. Wilt Thou let me remain in debt for my rent? I cannot believe it! Far in the great ocean of Thy creation, there are still many thousand fishes who might bring the money I need. Therefore, I beg Thee not to leave me in perplexity, but come and help." We gathered round listening and felt strangely moved, especially we students from the University, whose heads were full of the immutability of nature's laws and the impossibility of any deviation from her rules, together with many similarly wise notions.

"God's clock goes slowly, but correctly," says the proverb, and we were about to discover this truth. We separated; our mother and the girls busied themselves about the house, while we boys gathered in a confidential chat, all the while entertaining a sort of secret curiosity as to whether any results would follow that prayer. As the morning hours slipped by, we almost decided to give up our watch.

Shortly before noon, however, we were roused by a knock which heralded the entrance of the village pastor, a former friend of our father's, for whose sake he had always taken a hearty interest in our welfare. To our surprise, he had on his clerical robes. "Ah," said he, in answer to our inquiring looks, "I will soon tell you why I come thus. On my way to the prayer-meeting at church I was met by the postman, bringing a packet from the Dean of Leonberg. I opened it in the vestry, and found a note directing that the enclosed grant of money should be placed in the hands of Madame Paulus, being adjudged her from a charitable fund." The pastor went on to say that he could not tell through whose influence the grant had been accorded, having himself played no part in the matter. "But," he added, "as I knew the gift would be welcome,

I could not help running in with it on my way home, so as to share your joy." At this moment our mother entered the room, and the good man asked whether she could say how the grant came to be sent. "I forwarded a petition, Sir," she replied, "not to the dean, however, or indeed to any man at all, but to Him whose cabinet of exchange is established on high."

The kind pastor was visibly moved, and as for us, the tears stood in our eyes, and we all confessed that we had to-day gained a lesson, worth many hundred of our University lectures.

CHAPTER X.

The Happy Close.

Time passed quickly. Of our mother's elder sons, one had now become doctor at Kornthal, and taken her and our sisters to live with him; another assumed the direction of a chemical establishment at the same place, and a third had gone as tutor into Switzerland, when a proposal was made that he should undertake the superintendence of a seminary for boys at Kornthal. This offer was accepted as it presented a prospect of allowing the whole family to take part in the work, and thus accomplish a worthy task. My mother especially consented to the plan with joy, as she had always taken peculiar interest in training the young.

After vainly waiting several months for pupils, the number of boys suddenly multiplied to such an extent that our house became too small to hold them, whilst insuperable difficulties seemed to stand in the way of building another. Just at this juncture, when our way seemed hedged up on every side, a card reached us to found a similar institution near Ludwigsburg. We agreed, and were able to enter our new home with eighty pupils, in three months. The numbers shortly increased to more than a hundred. Over all these boys our mother watched with lively interest. Almost every evening, she might be found in one or other of the school-rooms, playing chess with the lads, or relating some story with a graphic power that drew crowds around her.

On these occasions, she sat amongst them

surrounded by the smallest ones, the remainder ranging themselves in an outer circle, whilst those who could not see her would climb on chairs and tables, so that anyone entering the room at first perceived only a towering throng of boys, and it required minute inspection before "the mother" could be discovered, buried in the midst of them. She also often attended at their out-door games and exercises, where her presence was hailed with delight. Frequently she undertook walking-tours of several days, on which she was accompanied by ten or twelve of the pupils, and those accounted themselves highly favored who were allowed to join her party; for her spirits were so gay and mirthful, that she imparted interest and life to all her surroundings.

The whole school called her *Mother*, and such

indeed she proved in tender love to all, both in good days and bad.

Thus life passed on for several years, and until it happened that one peculiarly cold winter the boys conceived the idea of building a snow fortress, which was to be assaulted and stormed. The day for this display had arrived, and the school was divided into two parties, the defenders and besiegers. The latter were to be declared victorious so soon as they should have placed their flag upon the high tower crowning the white edifice. Our mother, who took an active interest in these arrangements, espoused the cause of the assailants, whom she furnished with snow balls, cheering them to press on bravely and sturdily, never pausing till their colors should wave from the summit. "See," she cried, "that is just how it is with us! Each human heart is a fortress, which has been taken in possession by enemies, low, unworthy passions and vices: the grand point is for us to struggle without ceasing, till the flag of a better purpose, a new life, waves from the citadel!"

The struggle was a lengthy one that day, and untiringly she furnished the snowy weapons until at length the end was gained, the assailants made good their position, and planted their triumphal standard aloft, when loud shouts of victory rent the air, and seemed as if they would never cease.

But our good mother had been exposed too long, and the consequence was a violent chill, which developed into feverish symptoms the next day. She attached no importance to this indisposition, and on being asked by our doctor whether she expected to recover, merrily answered, "*Spero quod*" ("I hope so.") When left alone with her children she added, "This is sent to try your faith. If you pray earnestly, and believingly, I shall soon be well." We did all we could, but the illness continued to gain ground, and caused us fresh anxiety every day. In the course of the fourth night, she cried suddenly: "Children, you must pray earnestly, *much more earnestly;* kneel down together and ask God's help." This we did, praying aloud, but she exclaimed: "You do not understand," and raising herself, she folded her trembling hands, and said: "Lord, Thou knowest that I have not finished a great deal of the work which was begun on my knees there in the corner by the stove. Therefore I beg that my life may be somewhat lengthened. Once, when Thy servant Joshua could not complete his day's work, Thou didst, at his prayer, stop the course of sun and moon, those large heavenly bodies, so it must be only an easy thing for Thee to make my small body healthy and strong again, and give me time for what remains for me to do."

The words were hardly out of her lips, when she sank into a calm, deep slumber. We had long vainly hoped for this, and could not but trust that it might prove a favorable crisis in the malady, and that her prayer had been answered in peace. But upon awakening the next morning after several hours of quiet rest, she uttered the words, "Glory already! Children, it is ordered otherwise than we thought. I am going home! Come, we will once more celebrate the feast of our Savior's dying love together." We did so, and afterwards each of our number received her farewell kiss. Then she sank into the weakness of death, and slowly, but gently, the bonds of earth were loosed, and in unbroken heavenly peace her spirit passed away.

Our feelings as we watched her entrance into glory, may be expressed in the words:

"It is not exile, rest on high,
It is not sadness, peace from strife;
To fall asleep is not to die,
To rest with Christ is better life!"

CHAPTER XI.

In Memoriam.

So closes the "life-work" of one of the holiest, most energetic, and most faithful of women, whose ruling characteristic was self-forgetting devotedness and fervant love.

Need we wonder to be told, not only that her children and children's children rise up and call her blessed, but that the little country which gave her birth, though in her day numbering but a million of people, has sent out a large proportion of that noble band of foreign evangelists, whose deeds of undying fame have rendered our age memorable. The peasants who drank in spiritual life and energizing faith from such men as her father and grandfather, have given their hardy bodies and strong powerful minds, after due preparation, to go forth into many a dark region, there to sow broadcast the seed of that living Word, which in the retirement of their secluded villages had taken root in their own minds. And many a humble mother's heart, in that primitive country, has bounded with joy at the report of victories won for Christ by her son in the far-off fields of his trial and conflict.

The descendants of Madame Paulus still follow in the track marked out by her; honorably and usefully fulfilling their course, and educating in their large and prosperous Institution * both the sons of their own soil and youths sent them from all parts of Europe and the mission field.

* The Salon, near Ludwigsburg, Württemberg.

"He that trusteth in the Lord, mercy shall compass him about. Be glad in the Lord, and rejoice ye righteous; and shout for joy all ye that are upright in heart." 32 Ps. 10-11 v.

END.

www.ingramcontent.com/pod-product-compliance
Lightning Source LLC
LaVergne TN
LVHW021430110826
845150LV00007B/2164
* 9 7 8 1 4 2 5 5 0 6 8 7 2 *